Pre-reader

Puffins

Maya Myers

NATIONAL GEOGRAPHIC

Washington, D.C.

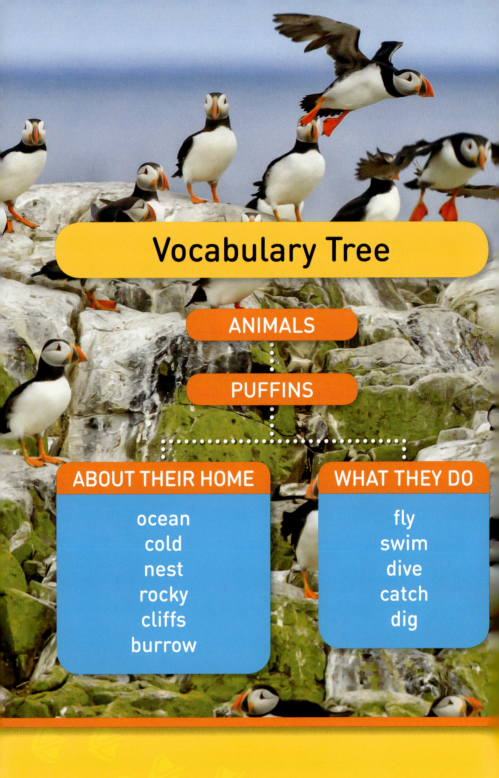

Vocabulary Tree

ANIMALS

PUFFINS

ABOUT THEIR HOME
ocean
cold
nest
rocky
cliffs
burrow

WHAT THEY DO
fly
swim
dive
catch
dig

Look at all these puffins!

Puffins live where the ocean is cold.

They make their nests on rocky cliffs.

Puffins use their wings to fly fast.

They can fly as fast as cars drive!

Puffins use their wings to swim. They dive to catch fish.

Their strong beaks can hold a lot of fish.

A puffin mom and dad bring fish to their baby.

A baby puffin
is called a puffling.

The puffling eats and eats.
It grows and grows.

After about six weeks, it is big enough to leave the nest.

13

Now the young puffin can find its own food.

As it grows, its beak, feet, and feathers change colors.

Now the puffin is an adult.

It finds a mate.
They will be a mom and dad.

Puffins make their nests in small caves called burrows.

They dig a burrow and make a nest.

The mom lays an egg in the nest.

The mom and dad take turns sitting on the egg.

Soon, a new puffling will hatch!

YOUR TURN!

Puffins can catch up to 12 fish in their beaks at once! How many "fish" can you catch?

- Find 12 socks and lay them out on the floor.
- Put your hands together and open and close them like a beak.
- Use your "beak" to pick up one sock at a time.
- Can you get them all without dropping any?

For my three pufflings —M.M.

The author and publisher gratefully acknowledge the expert content review of this book by Stephen W. Kress, Ph.D., executive director for the Seabird Restoration Program at the National Audubon Society (projectpuffin.audubon.org), and the literacy review of this book by Kimberly Gillow, Principal, Chelsea School District, Michigan.

Copyright © 2019 National Geographic Partners, LLC

Published by National Geographic Partners, LLC, Washington, D.C. 20036. All rights reserved. Reproduction in whole or in part without written permission of the publisher is prohibited.

NATIONAL GEOGRAPHIC and Yellow Border Design are trademarks of the National Geographic Society, used under license.

Designed by Gus Tello

Photo Credits
Cover, sigita playdon photography/Getty Images; 1, Wholelottarosy/Getty Images; 2–3, Robert Harding Picture Library/National Geographic Image Collection; 4–5, Life On White/Getty Images; 6–7, Noel Bennett/Getty Images; 8, Alex Mustard/2020 VISION/Nature Picture Library; 9, Bousfield/Getty Images; 10, Sebastian Wasek/Getty Images; 11, Mike Jones/Alamy Stock Photo; 12, Samuel R. Maglione/Science Source; 13, Leopardinatree/Getty Images; 14–15, Ralph Lee Hopkins/National Geographic Image Collection; 16–17, Johnny Giese/Shutterstock; 18, Alan Payton/Alamy Stock Photo; 19, Mike Jones/FLPA/Alamy Stock Photo; 20–21, Glen Bartley/Getty Images; 22 (UP LE), Rudmer Zwerver/Shutterstock; 22–23 (striped socks), Olga Popova/Shutterstock; 22–23 (long socks), Natan86/Shutterstock; 22–23 (short socks), paleka19/Getty Images; 24, Christoph Ruisz/Getty Images

Library of Congress Cataloging-in-Publication Data

Names: Myers, Maya, author. | National Geographic Society (U.S.)
Title: National Geographic readers : puffins / by Maya Myers.
Other titles: Puffins
Description: Washington, DC : National Geographic Kids, [2019] | Series: National Geographic readers Audience: Age 2-5. | Audience: Pre-school, excluding K.
Identifiers: LCCN 2018057778 (print) | LCCN 2018058866 (ebook) | ISBN 9781426335068 (e-book) | ISBN 9781426335075 (e-book + audio) | ISBN 9781426335044 (paperback) | ISBN 9781426335051 (hardcover)
Subjects: LCSH: Puffins--Juvenile literature.
Classification: LCC QL696.C42 (ebook) | LCC QL696.C42 M94 2019 (print) | DDC 598.3/3--dc23
LC record available at https://lccn.loc.gov/2018057778

National Geographic supports K–12 educators with ELA Common Core Resources. Visit natgeoed.org/commoncore for more information.

Printed in the United States of America
21/WOR/2